THE HAWAIIAN NAME BOOK

Hawaiian Translation

by Patrick Ka'ano'i
and
Robert Lokomaika'iokalani Snakenberg

Bess Press, Inc.
P.O. Box 22388
Honolulu, HI 96822

Dedicated to
David and Emily Ka'ano'i,
Aloha Mau Loa

Copyright © 1988 by the Bess Press, Inc.
ALL RIGHTS RESERVED
Printed in the United States of America

Library of Congress
CATALOG CARD NUMBER: 87-72563
 Honolulu, Hawai'i: Bess Press
 64 pages, English-Hawaiian
 ISBN: 0-935848-52-5

TABLE OF CONTENTS

Foreword................................. v

Preface................................. vii

Introduction............................. ix

How To Use This Book..................... xi

Writing and Pronounciation of Hawaiian.... xiii

Abbreviations........................... xv

Masculine-Kāne Names..................... 1

Feminine-Wahine Names................... 22

Bibliography............................ 43

PUBLISHER'S NOTE ON TYPOGRAPHY

Because of the type style of this book the diacritical mark called a *hamza* (‛) is rendered as an *apostrophe* ('), and may be used as its equivalent.

FOREWORD

The Hawaiian language teacher or the Hawaiian Studies program *kupuna* frequently has occasion to ask a child, " 'O wai kou inoa Hawai'i?" This means, "What is your Hawaiian name?" The child frequently has a beautiful name connoting aspects of nature or some human quality admired by the child's *'ohana*. Other times the child may answer with a name like Lopaka or Keoki or Kalolina. That's always a little sad, since these are merely Anglo-Saxon, Hebrew, Latin, or Celtic names that have been pronounced in the Hawaiian way over the generations with many people accepting them as "Hawaiian" names now.

The best way, of course, to get a real Hawaiian name is to ask a family *kupuna* or elder to bestow a name upon the beloved child. Often this is not possible for increasing numbers of families in Hawai'i, both Hawaiian and non-Hawaiian. These true Hawaiian names might be those passed down from antiquity in the family, names dreamed during sleep, or names crafted to describe some favorite aspect of our Hawaiian environment.

This little book does not in any way purport to take the place of the traditional name-giving process in Hawai'i. It does, however, hope to provide readers with some options to giving names that are not merely transliterated or Hawaiianized from common English and other names.

It was fascinating to discover the actual meaning of many of the names we just take for granted in our time. The Hebrew names, of which there are *kū ka paila* (plenty) in this book, were actually complete sentences which translate to rather long, ungainly names in Hawaiian. Even if the translations are not used to name someone, at least the reader will learn what these common names mean and how to express them in Hawaiian.

The authors hope that this book will be understood and used in the sentiment of *aloha* with which it is offered to provide greater knowledge and appreciation of our beautiful *'ōlelo makuahine* or mother tongue.

Robert Lokomaika'iokalani Snakenberg
Maunalua, Honolulu, Hawai'i

PREFACE

The genesis of this book was born out of a family discussion in 1982. One of my brothers was very critical about my daughter having a Hawaiian first name. His concern was centered on the effect her Hawaiian first name, Mālialani, would have on non-Hawaiian children in school. He was afraid it would be difficult to pronounce and would draw attention to her Hawaiian identity, a concern, as I would discover, not maintained exclusively by my brother.

It was true not one of my family members, friends, or acquaintances bore a Hawaiian first name; in my family my daughter was the first. Many had Hawaiian middle names, but a Christian first name seemed to have an exclusive place among Hawaiian people.

A Law of 1860

Why a Christian name instead of a Hawaiian first name? This question led me to discover a law signed by Kamehameha IV in 1860 exclusively mandating that a Christian first name be given to all children born in Hawai'i. This law remained in effect until 1967.

The effect of this law would create a whole listing of Hawaiian pronunciations, or *Hawaiianized* forms of Christian first names; in some instances the *Hawaiianized* form of a Christian first name was used as a last name as well.

A New Era

Around the early 1970s a great awakening in Hawaiian identity gained public attention. This evolved into an ever increasing scrutiny of Hawaiian self-identity and desire to express the positive beauty of things Hawaiian, especially in the use of one's Hawaiian name.

The giving of a Hawaiian name, traditionally, comes from one's Hawaiian speaking *kūpuna*, Hawaiian elders. This traditional source of Hawaiian name giving is greatly sought after but regrettably not easily obtainable, due to the diminished number of Hawaiian speaking *kūpuna*.

A New Source

Since the resurgence of Hawaiian identity and language, a continuing contribution of written works is helping Hawaiians and the community at large enrich the source of things Hawaiian.

This book is a direct result of the need to have an added source of Hawaiian names translated from the meaning of most used given names.

The Style of Translation

Because of the subjective nature of translations, the following guide was used for the philosophy and style of translation used in this book.

1. Names should not be Hawaiianized.
2. Names should be euphonic, sound pleasing to the ear.
3. Names should be rendered as one or two word translations where possible.
4. Names should not have negative connotations.
5. Names should have diacritical marks where applicable.

Acknowledgments

A very special *mahalo nui loa* to Lokomaika'iokalani Snakenberg. His contributing expertise in Hawaiian language and aloha for this work have been major contributions. Also to my wife Heinke for her love, inspiration and support.

Closing Note

The research, study and application of this book has been a rich and rewarding exerience especially in the field of genealogy, where it has enlightened me on the *kaona*, or hidden meanings, of my first and last names.

Names are living treasures of your identity. I hope this book offers insight and inspiration. Carry and wear your names well.

      Aloha,

      Patrick Ka'ano'i
      Honolulu, Hawai'i

INTRODUCTION

Purpose Of This Book

The Hawaiian Name Book is a dictionary of most used first names with their meanings and origins as translated into Hawaiian.

The purpose of this book is to give true Hawaiian translations of non-Hawaiian given names and offer an alternative to the familiar *Hawaiianized* spellings and pronunciations of non-Hawaiian given names.

This book is also a resource of true Hawaiian names and offers individuals and parents-to-be a more meaningful understanding of their names and help in giving names to their children.

As simple as the purpose of this book may be, up till now, no popular work of this kind has been offered. What are *Hawaiianized* names and why is there a popularity of Christian first names in Hawai'i? Following is an explanation of what *Hawaiianized* means and a brief history of the origin of Christian name giving in Hawai'i.

Hawaiianized Spelling and Pronunciation

Hawaiianized means "to give a Hawaiian form, style or idiom." Following are two examples of masculine names that were *Hawaiianized*. They are a product of the Hawaiian style of pronunciation and transliteration, the form of representing a sound in one language by alphabetical characters of another language.

For example:
> The names JIM and GEORGE would be *Hawaiianized* into KIMO and KEOKI respectively. JIM is *Hawaiianized* by substituting the sound of the letter K for J. The sounds of the letters I and M exist in both languages so they are retained and the vowel sound O is added at the end. GEORGE is *Hawaiianized* by substituting the sound of the letter K for G; the sound of the letters E and O remain the same. The sound R was originally and is still dropped in the New England-inspired Hawaiian pronunciation of English, the sound of the letter G is substituted

by the letter K, and the letter E, in this case, is substituted by the letter I.

```
JIM:  J - K        GEORGE:  G - K
      I - I                 E - E
      M - M                 O - O
        - O                 R   (dropped)
                            G - K
                            E - I
```

Since Hawaiian words all end in a vowel, all *Hawaiianized* words must also end in a vowel.

For more details on this process, see Elbert and Pūku'i, *Hawaiian Grammar,* pages 27-33.

Why Christian Names?

The *Hawaiianized* form of Christian name giving was initiated by a law, signed by Kamehameha IV, August 24, A.D. 1860, that declared all children shall have a surname and 'They shall, besides, have a Christian name suitable to their sex.' This law remained in effect until April 5, 1967, when it was "... amended by the deletion of the words 'Christian name suitable to their sex' therein and the substitution of the words 'given name' therefor." (H.B. 117., Act 6)

This was the official reason for the popularity of Christian first names and the use of Hawaiianized Christian names.

HOW TO USE THIS BOOK

Choosing A Hawaiian Name

When choosing a Hawaiian name you may use both the masculine-*kāne* and feminine-*wahine* Hawaiian listings for either sex. There are very few self-explanatory feminized or masculinized Hawaiian translations.

Because of the simple order of text the reader may scan the listings by meaning, which follow just after the Hawaiian translation.

The Hawaiian philosophy of choosing names is a very thoughtful one and should be studied carefully for positive meanings that may contribute to the purpose and dignity of the bearer's lifetime and beyond.

Order Of Text Entry

This dictionary is divided into two sections: first a listing, in alphabetical order, of masculine names, and then a listing of feminine names.

Given names are listed first; then the Hawaiian translation; followed by the given name's meaning in English and the origins of the given name, abbreviated, in parentheses. For example, masculine listing: AARON — Mālamalama, Shining. (H) Refer to the listing of 'Abbreviations Used In This Dictionary' for origins of names. In this case (H) means of Hebrew origin.

Qualified Translations

In some cases the Hawaiian translation is qualified in parentheses ( ). For example, masculine listing: DEXTER — No'eau (Skillful) Right handed; fortunate, skillful, (L)

Omitted Name Translations

In a few cases, some common names were not included because their meaning had no equivalent in the Hawaiian language. For example:
    MAGDALENE, Woman of Magdala. (H)
    INGRID, Ing's ride. (Gmc.)

There are no Hawaiian equivalents to the words Magdala or Ing (a god in Germanic mythology).

Diminutive and Variant Spellings

Throughout these listings you will encounter the abbreviations, *var.* and *dim. Var.* stands for *variant,* and means 'a different spelling, pronunciation or form of the same word.' *Dim.* stands for *diminutive,* sometimes referred to as 'a pet name.' Diminutive means 'a word formed from another to express diminished size.' Whenever a variation *var.* or diminished *dim.* form is expressed, refer to the original name for the translation, meaning, and origin.

Sometimes you will find a few forms of the name before you obtain the original name.

For example, masculine listing:
    CARY Dim. of Carol.
    CAROL English form of Carolus.
    CAROLUS Latin form of Charles.
    CHARLES — Kūkāne, Manly. (F,G)

Feminine From Masculine Names

The female listing will commonly refer to the masculine origin of that name; refer to the masculine listing and use the male-female Hawaiian translation.

For example, female listing:
    CLEMENTINE Fem. of Clement.

From the masculine listing:
    CLEMENT — Alohalani, Merciful. (L)

WRITING AND PRONUNCIATION OF HAWAIIAN

Along with the 12 letters of the Hawaiian alphabet, A, E, H, I, K, L, M, N, O, P, U, W, there are two diacritical markers: a macron (*kahakō* in Hawaiian), a straight line (-) over a vowel that represents a long sound as in (ā); and a hamza (*'okina* in Hawaiian) which is an Arabic character (') to represent a glottal stop. When writing in Hawaiian the diacritical markers should be included. They are critical components of the pronunciation of the Hawaiian word and can dramatically alter the meaning of that word. For example:

pau   to end, finish.   pa'ū   moist, damp, moldy.
pa'u soot or drudgery.   pā'ū   wrap around garment.

Consonants

p, k similar to English but with less aspiration.
h, l, m, n as in English
w after *i* and *e* usually like *v*; after *u* and *o* usually *w*; initially and after *a* like *v* or *w*.
' a glottal stop, similar to the sound between the oh's in English oh-oh.

Vowels

Unstressed	Stressed
a like *a* in above	ā like *a* in far
e like *e* in bet	ē like *ay* in play
i like *y* in city	ī like *ee* in see
o like *o* in sole	ō like *o* in sole
u like *oo* in moon	ū like *oo* in moon

Rising Diphthongs

ei, eu, oi, ou, ai, ae, ao, au

These are always stressed on the first member, but the two members are not as closely joined as in English.

For more details on pronunciation of Hawaiian, see Elbert-Pūku'i, *Hawaiian Grammar*.

ABBREVIATIONS USED IN THIS DICTIONARY

AF Anglo-French (1050 A.D. to 1475)
Ar. Aramaic
Arb. Arabic
C Celtic
Dan. Danish
dim. diminutive
Du. Dutch
Egypt. Egyptian
E English
F French
fem. feminine
G German
Glc. Gaelic
Gk. Greek
Gmc. Germanic
H Hebrew
Haw. Hawaiian
Itl. Italian
L Latin
masc. masculine
ME Middle English (1050 A.D. to 1475)
MI Middle Irish (110 A.D. to 1600)
NL New Latin (After 1500 A.D.)
Norw. Norwegian
OE Old English (450 A.D. to 1050)
OF Old French (850 A.D. to 1400)
Per. Persian
Pg. Portuguese
Russ. Russian
Scand. Scandinavian
Scot. Scottish
Skt. Sanskrit
Sp. Spanish
Sw. Swedish
var. variant
Wel. Welsh

MASCULINE — Kāne

A

AARON — Mālamalama, Shining. (H)

ABEL — Kahanu, Breath. (H)

ABRAHAM — Makuaokalehulehu, Father of a mighty nation.(H)

ADOLPH — ʻĪliohaealiʻi, Noble wolf. (G)

ADRIAN — Waiwai, Rich. (Gk.)

ALAN — Nohea, Handsome. (C)

ALBERT — ʻAlohilani, Nobly bright. (F)

ALEXANDER — Kapalekanaka, Defender of men. (Gk.)

ALFRED — Naʻauao, Wise. (OE)

ALPHONSO — ʻOhanaaliʻi, Noble family. (G)

ALVIN — Hoaaliʻi, Noble friend. (G)

AMOS — Mauhaʻalina, To be burdened. (H)

ANDREW — Kūkāne, Manly. (Gk.)

ANTHONY — Lupalupa, Flourishing. (Gk.)

ARCHIBALD — Koalani, Nobly bold. (G)

ARNOLD — Aliʻihanohano, Honorable ruler. (G)

ARTHUR — Puʻuʻiuʻiu, Lofty hill. (Glc.)

ASHLEY — Kulaʻōlena, Ash tree meadow. (OE)

AUBREY — Aliʻinaʻauao, Wise ruler, from High German Alberic. (G)

AUGUSTINE Same as Augustus.

AUGUSTUS — Mōʻiuʻiu, Venerable, exalted. (L)

AVERY — Var. of Aubrey. (AS)

B

BALDWIN — Hoaalohakoa, Bold friend. (G)

BALTHAZAR — Kalanikamahoi (The splendid noble), Splendid prince. (Per.)

BAPTIST — Kahoʻohānauhou, Baptiser. (Gk.)

BARNABAS — Kamakāneho'opaipai, Son of exhortation. (Gk., L, Ar.)

BARNARD Var. of Bernard.

BARNEY Dim. of Barnabas or Bernard.

BARRY — Kaihe, Spear. (C)

BARTHOLOMEW — Mōʻali (Furrows), Son of Furrows. (Ar.)

BASIL — Hoʻāliʻi, Kingly. (Gk.)

BAXTER — Kahoʻokālua, Baker. (OE)

BENEDICT — Pōmaikaʻi, Blessed. (L)

BENJAMIN — Punahele (Favorite), Son of the right hand; favorite. (H)

BENNET Var. of Benedict.

BERT Dim. of Albert, Bertram, Gilbert, Herbert, and Hubert.

BERTRAM — Kaulana, Famous. (G)

BILL Dim. of William.

BOB Dim. of Robert.

BORIS — Kekoa, Warrior. (Russ.)

BOYD — Lauohomelemele, Yellow-haired. (C)

BRIAN — Hoʻolua, Strong. (C)

BRICE — Keliʻi, Rich, noble, powerful. (C)

BRUCE — Kapuoʻa, Woods or thicket. (Scot.)

BRUNO — Kamākuʻe, The brown one. (G)

BURGESS — Kekupa, Citizen. (G)

BYRON — Haleiki, Cottage. (G)

C

CAESAR — Keliʻi, Royalty. (L)

CAIN — Loaʻa, Acquire, possess. (H)

CALVIN — ʻŌhule, Bald. (L)

CARL English form of Karl. See Charles.

CAROL English form of Carolus. See Charles.

CAROLUS Latin form of Charles.

CARY Dim. of Carol. See Charles.

CASPER — Kalanikiakahi (Supreme chief), Imperial. (G) Also Caspar.

CECIL — Makapō, Blind. (L)

CEDRIC — 'Alihikaua (General), War chief. (C)

CHARLES — Kūkāne, Manly. (F, G)

CHAUNCEY — Kamālamamo'oleloali'i, Keeper of royal records. (OF)

CHESTER — Kahua, Fortress or camp. (L)

CHRISTIAN — Kahaiāokaponia, Follower of the anointed one. (L)

CHRISTOPHER — Kameahi'iokaponia, Bearer of the annointed one, Bearer of Christ. (Gk.)

CLARENCE — Kaulana, Illustrious. (L)

CLAUDE — 'O'opa, Lame. (L)

CLAY — Pālolo, Clay, to stick together. (G, Indo-European)

CLAYTON Var. of Clay.

CLEMENT — Alohalani, Merciful. (L)

CLIFFORD — Ala'aumakapali, Crossing/ford by a cliff. (E)

CLIFTON — Mahina'aimakapali, Farm by the cliff. (E)

CLINTON — Kūlanakauhalemakapu'u, Town on a hill. (E)

CLIVE — Kapali, Cliff. (E)

CLYDE — Lohemamao, Heard from afar. (Wel.)

COLIN — Manukū, Dove. (Scot.)

CONRAD — A'okoa, Bold counsel. (G)

CONSTANT Var. of Constantine.

CONSTANTINE — Kūpa'a, Constant, firm. (L)

CORNELIUS — Kiwiakalā, Horn of the sun. (L)

CRAIG — Noho'āpali, Crag dweller. (Scot.)

CRISPIN — Lauohomimilo, Curly headed. (L)

CURTIS — 'Olu'olu, Courteous. (OF)

CUTHBERT — Naʻauaokaulana, Notably brilliant. (OF)
CYRIL — Kūhaku, Lordly. (Gk.)
CYRUS — Kalā, The sun. (Per.)

D

DAN — Lunakānāwai, Judge. (H)

DANIEL — ʻOkeakuakoʻulunakānāwai, God is my judge. (H)

DARIUS — Waiwai, Wealthy. (Pers.)

DARRYL — Kaululāʻau (The grove), Grove of oak trees. (E)

DAVID — ʻAnoʻi, Beloved. (H)

DEAN — Alakaʻi, Leader. (OF)

DEMETRIUS — Alohaʻāina, Lover of the earth. (Gk.)

DENNIS Var. of Dionysius.

DEREK Dim. of Theodoric.

DEXTER — Noʻeau (Skillful), Right handed, fortunate, skillful. (L)

DICK Dim. of Richard.

DIEGO Spanish form of James.

DIONYSIUS — Aliʻileʻa, God of wine and revelry. (Gk.)

DOLPH Dim. of Adolph or Rudolph.

DOMINIC — Nokahaku, Of the Lord. (L)

DONALD — Aliʻihaʻaheo, Proud ruler. (C)

DOUGLAS — ʻĀhina, Gray. (C)

DREW Dim. of Andrew.

DUANE Var. of Wayne. (E)

DUDLEY — Kulamauʻu (Meadow), Doddʻs meadow. (OE).

DUKE — Alakaʻi, Leader. (L)

DUNCAN — Koaʻilimākuʻe, Dark skinned warrior. (C)

DUNSTAN — Luaʻelipōhakuʻula, Brown rock quarry. (OE)

DUSTIN Var. of Dunstan.

DWIGHT — Kekea; White, fair. (OE)

E

EARL — Kekoa, Warrior. (OE)

EBENEZER — Pōhakukihi, Cornerstone. (H)

EDGAR — Koapōmaika'i, Fortunate warrior. (OE)

EDMUND — Kia'iwaiwai, Rich protector. (OE)

EDWARD — Kahuwaiwai, Rich guardian. (OE)

EDWIN — Hoaalohawaiwai, Rich friend. (OE)

EGBERT — Pahi'alohi, Bright sword. (OE)

ELBERT Var. of Albert.

ELDRED — Kuauhāna'auao, Wise counsel. (OE)

ELEAZAR — Kōkuako'uakua, My God has helped. (H)

ELIAS Var. of Elijah.

ELIHU Var. of Elijah.

ELIJAH — 'Okahakuko'uakua, The Lord is my God. (H)

ELIOT Var. of Elijah

ELISHA — 'Okeolako'uakua, God is salvation. (H)

ELMER — Kaulana, Famous. (OE)

ELROY — Kalani, Royal, king. (L)

ELTON — Kūlanakauhalekahiko, Possibly meaning 'old town.' (E)

ELVIN — Hoakūakua, Godly friend. (OE)

EMANUEL — 'Okeakuapūmemākou, God is with us. (H) var. of Immanuel.

EMERY — Pa'ahana, Industrious. (G)

EMILE — Pa'ahana, Industrious. (L) Also Emil.

EMMETT — Naonao, Ant. (OE)

EMMETT — 'Oia'i'o, Truth. (H)

ENEAS — Kūikamahalo, Praiseworthy. (Gk)

ENOCH — La'ahia, Dedicated. (H)

ENOS — Kāne, Man. (H)

ENRICO Italian form of Henry.

EPHRAIM — Huahua, Fruitful. (H)

ERASMUS — Hoʻālohaloha, Lovable. (Gk.)
ERASTUS — Hoʻālohaloha, Lovable. (Gk.)
ERIC — Keliʻihanohano, Honorable king. (Scand.)
ERMANO Italian form of Herman.
ERNEST — Kūpaʻa, Earnest, resolute. (G)
ERWIN Var. of Irving.
ESTEBAN Spanish form of Stephen.
ETHAN — Ikaika, Strong. (H)
ETHELBERT — ʻAlohilani, Nobly bright. (OE)
ETHELRED — ʻAhaʻula, Noble council. (G)
ETIENNE French form of Stephen.
EUGENE — Hānaupōmaikaʻi, Well-born. (Gk.)
EUSTACE — ʻOhimaikaʻi, Good harvest. (Gk.)
EVAN Welsh form of John.
EVELYN Masc. of Eve. (H)
EVERARD Var. of Everett.
EVERETT — Puaʻakeʻa, Boar. (OE)
EZEKIEL — Hoʻoikaikakeakua, God strengthens. (H)
EZRA — Kōkua, Help. (H)

F

FEDOR Russian form of Theodore.
FELIPE Spanish form of Phillip.
FELIX — Hauʻoli, Happy. (L)
FERDINAND — Koamalu, Peaceful courage. (G)
FERGUS — Ikaikakūkāne, Manly strength. (C)
FELIPO Italian form of Phillip.
FLOYD Var. of Lloyd.
FRANCIS — Kanakakūʻokoʻa, Freeman. (ME)
FRANK Dim. of Francis or Franklin.
FRANKLIN — Kanakakūʻokoʻa (Freeman), Freeholder. (OE)
FRED Dim. of Alfred, Frederick, or Wilfred.

FREDERICK — Aliʻimalu, Peaceful ruler. (G)

FRITZ Dim. of Frederick.

G

GABRIEL — ʻOkeakuakoʻuikaika, God is my strength. (H)

GAMALIEL — Makanaakua, Reward of God. (H)

GARDINER — Mahiʻai, Gardener. (Gmc.)

GARRET Var. of Gerard.

GARY Dim. of Garret.

GASPAR Var. of Casper.

GAUTIER French form of Walter.

GENE Dim. of Eugene.

GEOFFREY — Maluokeakua, God's peace. (OE)

GEORGE — Mahiʻai, Earthworker, farmer. (Gk.)

GERALD — Kekoalaweihe, Spearbearer. (G)

GERRARD — Kekoalaweihe, Spearbearer. (G)

GERONIMO Italian form of Jerome.

GIACOMO Italian form of James.

GIDEON — Kekoanui, Mighty warrior. (H)

GIERONYMUS Latin form of Jerome.

GIFFORD — Makanakūpono, Worthy gift. (ME)

GILBERT — Malamaokalehulehu, Light of many. (OE)

GILES — Pale, Shield. (Gk.)

GIOVANI Italian form of John.

GIULIO Italian form of Julius.

GIUSEPPE Italian form of Joseph.

GLENN — Awāwaiki, Glen, a small valley. (Scot.)

GODDARD — Kūpaʻalani, Divine resoluteness. (G)

GODFREY — Maluhialani, Divinely peaceful. (G)

GODWIN — Hoaakua, Friend of God. (OE)

GORDON — Kameʻe, Hero. (Glc.)

GRAHAM — Haleʻāhina, Gray home. (OE)

GRANT — Hā'awi, To give, to grant. (OF)

GREGORY — Maka'ala, Vigilant. (Gk.)

GRIFFIN Var. of Griffith.

GRIFFITH — Lauoho'ula (For Caucasians), Lauoho'ehu (For Polynesians); Red-haired. (C)

GROVER — Mahiulula'au, A grower of trees. (OE)

GUALTERIO Spanish form of Walter.

GUGLIEIMO Italian form of William

GUIDO Italian form of Guy.

GUILLAUME French form of William.

GUILLERMO Spanish form of William.

GUS Dim. of Augustus or Gustavus.

GUSTAVUS — Ko'oko'omana (Staff of power), Goth's staff. (G)

GUY — Alaka'i, Guide. (OF)

H

HAL Dim. of Harold or Henry.

HAMILTON — Kauhale, Home. (OE)

HANK Dim. of Henry.

HANNIBAL — Pu'ukūnihi, Steep hill. (E)

HANS German dim. of Johannes. See John.

HARLEY — Kīhāpaiolonā, Field of hemp plants. (OE).

HAROLD — 'Alihikaua, Chief of the army. (OE)

HARRY Dim. of Harold or var. of Henry.

HARVEY — Kaua, Army battle. (G)

HECTOR — Heleuma, Anchor. (Gk.)

HENRY — Kahakuokahale, Ruler of the home. (OE)

HERBERT — Kekoapo'okela, Excellent soldier. (OE)

HERMAN — Kekoa, Soldier. (G)

HERMES — Ka'eleleonālani, The messenger of the gods. (Gk.)

HERNANDO Spanish form of Ferdinand.

HEZEKIAH — Ho'oikaikakeakua, God strengthens. (H)

HILARY — Hau'oli, Joyful. (L)

HIRAM — Ka'iu, Lofty, exalted. (H)

HOBART Var. of Hubert.

HODGE Dim. of Roger.

HOMER — Ho'ohiki, Pledge. (Gk.)

HONORE — Hanohano, Honored. (F)

HORACE — 'Ike, To see, to behold. (G)

HORATIO Italian form of Horace.

HOSEA — Keolamauloa, Salvation. (H)

HOWARD — Kia'iokekaua, Guardian of the army. (OE)

HUBERT Var. of Herbert.

HUGH Dim. of Hubert.

HUMBERT — Hale'alohi, Bright home. (G)

HUMPHREY — Kia'iokahale, Protector of the home. (OE)

I

IAN Scottish form of John.

ICHABOD — Hanohano'ole, Inglorious. (H)

IGNATIUS — Liholiho, Fiery. (Gk.)

IMMANUEL — 'Okeakuapūmemākou, God is with us. (H)

INIGO Var. of Ignatius.

IOSIF Russian form of Joseph.

IRA — Pakele, To escape. (Arb.)

IRVIN — Nohea, Handsome. (Glc.)

IRVING Var. of Irvin.

IRWIN Var. of Irving.

ISAAC — 'Aka, Laughter. (H)

ISAIAH — 'Okeakuakeola, God is salvation. (H)

ISIDORE — Makanaohina (Gift of Hina, Hawaiian moon goddess), Gift of Isis, Egyptian moon goddess. (Gk.)

ISRAEL — Paomoniikeakua, Contender with God. (H)

IVAN Russian form of John.

IVOR — Nihopalaoa, Ivory. (L)

J

JABEZ — Kaumaha, Sorrow. (H)

JACK English form of the French Jacques; dim. of John.

JACOB — Hoʻoilina, Successor. (H)

JACQUES French form of Jacob.

JAMES Var. of Jacob.

JAN German, Dutch form of John.

JANOS Hungarian form of John.

JAPHETH — Kanani, Beautiful. (H)

JARED — Kamamo, Descendant (H)

JARVIS — Kanaʻi, Conqueror. (OE)

JASON — Hoʻōla, Healer. (Gk.) Also a var. of Joshua.

JASPER — Hunapūlamaʻia, Treasured secret. (Per.) Also a stone.

JAY — Hauʻoli, Happy. (OE)

JEAN French form of John.

JEFFREY Var. of Geoffrey.

JEHU — Olakeakua, God lives. (H)

JEPHTHAN — Hāmama, Be opened. (H)

JEREMIAH — Hoʻālakeakua, God raises up. (H)

JEROME — Inoakapu, Sacred name. (Gk.)

JERRY Dim. of Jeremiah, Gerald, Gerard, or Jerome.

JESSE — Makana, Gift. (H)

JESUS Var. of Yehoshua.

JETHRO — Nāwaiwai, Riches. (H)

JIM Dim. of James.

JOAB — ʻOluʻolukeakua, God is willing. (H)

JOACHIM — Hoʻonohokeakua, God will establish. (H)

JOAO Portuguese form of John.

JOB — Hoʻomāino, Oppressed. (H)

JOCK Scottish form of Jack.

JOE Dim. of Joseph.

JOEL — 'Okeakuakahaku, The lord is God. (H)

JOHN English form of Yochanan.

JON Var. of John, Dim. of Jonathan.

JONAH — Manukū, Dove. (H)

JONATHAN — Makanaakua, Gift of God. (H)

JORGE Portuguese and Spanish form of George.

JOSEPH English form of Yosef.

JOSHUA Var. of Yehoshua.

JOSIAH — Keahiokahaku, Fire of the lord. (H)

JOTHAM — Hemolelekeakua, God is perfection. (H)

JUAN Spanish form of John.

JUDAH — Mililani, Praise. (H)

JULES French form of Julius.

JULIAN — 'Ōpiopio, Youthful. (Gk.)

JULIUS Var. of Julian.

JUSTIN Var. of Justus.

JUSTUS — Kūpono, Just, honest. (L)

K

KARL German form of Charles.

KASPAR German form of Jasper.

KEITH — Kamakani, Wind. (Scot)

KELVIN — Kameālohamoku, Lover of ships. (C)

KENNETH — Nohea, Handsome. (C)

KENT Var. of Kenneth.

KEVIN — Nohea, Handsome. (C)

KIT Dim. of Christopher.

KONRAD German form of Conrad.

L

LABAN Var. of Lavan.

LAFAYETTE — Paulele, Faith. (OF)

LAMBERT — 'Alohi'āina, Brightness of land. (F, G)

LANCE — Kaihemāmā, Light spear. (G)

LANCELOT French dim. of Lance.

LARS Swedish form of Laurence.

LAURENCE — Leiali'i, Crown. (L)

LAVAN — Kekea, White. (H)

LAWRENCE Var. of Laurence.

LAZARUS — Kōkuakeakua, God has helped. (H)

LEANDER — Makoa, Courageous. (Gk.)

LEE — Kīhāpai, Field. (OE)

LEICESTER — Kahuamalu, Protected camp area. (OE)

LEIF — Aloha'ia, Loved one. (Scand.)

LEIGH Var. of Lee.

LEMUEL — Nokeakua, Belonging to God. (H)

LEO — Makoa; Courageous, as a lion. (L)

LEON — Makoa; Courageous, as a lion. (L)

LEONARD — Ikaikaloa; Very strong, as a lion. (G)

LEONIDAS Var. of Leo.

LEOPOLD — Kapalekanaka, The defender of people. (G)

LEROY — Kalani, Royal. (OF)

LESLIE — Kulamau'u, Meadowland. (OE)

LESTER Var. of Leicester.

LEVI — Kāpili'ia, Joined. (H)

LEWIS Var. of Louis.

LINCOLN — Ka'olu; Supple, as a linden tree. (OE)

LINUS — Hākeakea; Blond, as linen colored. (Gk.)

LION — Heikaikako'u, I have strength. (H)

LIONEL Var. of Lion.

LISLE Var. of Lyle.

LLEWELLYN — Kamakoāli'i; Noble courage, as of a lion. (Wel.)

LLOYD — Ka'ilimāku'e, The dark skinned one. (Wel.)

LORENZO Var. of Laurence.

LOT — Kīpo'i'ia, Covered over. (H)

LOUIS — Kaulanaikekaua, Famous in battle. (OF)

LOWELL — Aloha'ia, Beloved. (E)

LUCAS Var. of Lucius.

LUCIAN Var. of Lucius.

LUCIFER — Pa'alama, Light-bearer. (L)

LUCIUS — Malama, Light. (L)

LUCRETIUS — Waiwai, Wealthy. (L)

LUKE English form of Lucas.

LUTHER — Koakaulana, Famous warrior. (G)

LYLE — Kamoku, The island. (OF)

LYMAN — Hamopuna, Plasterer. (OE)

LYNN — Kahawai, Brook. (OE)

M

MACK — Hana, To make. (G)

MALACHI — Ko'u'elele, My messenger. (H)

MALCOLM — Manukū, Dove. (Arb.)

MANUEL Short form of Immanuel.

MARCELLUS Dim. of Marcus.

MARCUS — Makekau; Warlike, as the Roman god Mars. (L)

MARION Masc. form of Mary.

MARK English form of Marcus.

MARSHAL — Ilāmuku, Executive officer. (G)

MARTIN Var. of Marcus.

MARVIN — Kahoaokekai, Friend of the sea. (OE)

MASON — Kālaipōhaku, Stoneworker. (OE)

MATTHEW — Makanaakua, Gift of God. (H)

MATTHIAS Var. of Matthew.

MAURICE — Kaʻilimākuʻe; Dark skinned, as a Moor.(G, L, ME)

MAX Dim. of Maximilian.

MAXIMILIAN — Kaulana, Famous. (L)

MAYNARD — Ikaika, Strong. (G)

MELVIN — Keliʻi; Leader, chief. (C)

MEREDITH — Keliʻinui, Great chief. (Wel.)

MERVIN Var. of Marvin.

MICAH Var. of Michael.

MICHAEL — ʻOwaikahoʻākua, "Who is like God?" (H)

MIKLOS Hungarian form of Nicholas.

MILES — Kekoa, Warrior. (Gk., L) English dim. of Michael.

MILO Italian var. of Miles.

MILTON — Kūlanakauhalewili, Mill town. (OE)

MITCHELL Var. of Michael.

MONROE — ʻOlokaʻa, To roll on a wheel. (L, F, Scot.)

MONTAGUE — Maunaʻoi; French form of the Latin, 'pointed mountain.'

MONTGOMERY Var. of Montague.

MORGAN — Nohokai, Sea dweller. (C)

MORRIS Var. of Maurice.

MORTIMER — Nohokai, Sea dweller. (AF)

MORTON — Kūlanakauhalekai, Sea town. (OE)

MOSES English form of Moshe.

MOSHE — Huleia, Drawn out (of the water). (H)

MOSHE — Kamakāne, Son. (Egypt.)

MURDOCK — Holomoku, Seaman. (C)

MURRAY — Holomoku, Seaman. (C, Wel.)

MYLES Var. of Miles.

N

NAHUM — Hōʻolu, To console. (H)

NAPOLEON — Kūlanakauhalehou, New town. (F)

NATHAN — Makana, Gift. (H)

NATHANIEL Var. of Netanel.

NECHEMYA — Hōʻoluʻiaekahaku, Comforted of the Lord. (H)

NED Dim. of Edgar, Edmund, or Edward.

NEHEMIAH Var. of Nechmya.

NEAL — Poʻokela, Champion. (C)

NEIL Var. of Neal.

NELSON — Kamakāneakapoʻokela (Son of a Champion), Nealʻs son. (ME, Glc.)

NERO — Ikaika, Strong. (L)

NETANEL — Makanaakua, Gift of God. (H)

NEVILLE — Kūlanakauhalehou, New town. (F)

NEWTON — Kūlanakauhalehou, New town. (OE)

NICHOLAS — Kalanakilaokalāhui, The peopleʻs victory. (Gk)

NIGEL — Keliʻi, Noble. (C)

NOACH — Kamaha, Rest. (H)

NOAH English form of Noach.

NOEL — Lāhānau, Birthday. (OF)

NORBERT — ʻAlohilani, Divine brightness. (G)

NORMAN — Kāneʻakau, Northman. (Scand.)

O

OBADIAH English form of Ovadya.

OCTAVIUS — Kawalu, The eighth (born). (L)

ODYSSEUS — Huakaʻi, Journey. (Gk.)

OLAF — Kupuna, Ancestor. (Scand.)

OLIVER — Kānehoʻomalu, Man of peace. (F)

ORLAND — ʻĀinamelemele, Golden land. (L)

ORLANDO Italian form of Orland.

OSBERT — 'Alohilani, Divine brilliance. (OE)
OSCAR — Ikaikalani, Divine strength. (OE)
OSMOND — Malulani, Divine protection. (OE)
OSWALD — Keakuaokanahele, God of the forest. (OE)
OTTO — Waiwai, Rich. (G)
OVADYA — Lawelaweokeakua, Servant of God. (H)
OWEN — Koa'ōpio, Young warrior. (Wel.)
OZ — Ikaika, Strength. (H)
OZZIE Dim. of Oswald.

P

PADRAIC Irish form of Patrick.
PATRICK — Mamoali'i; Patrician, noble descent. (L)
PAUL — Li'ili'i, Small. (H)
PERCEVAL — Pahuawāwa, Valley piercer. (OF)
PERCIVAL English form of Perceval.
PERCY Dim. of Percival.
PERRY French form of Peter.
PETER — Pōhaku, Rock. (Gk., L)
PHILANDER — Kānealoha, Loving man. (Gk.)
PHILEMON — Aloha, Loving. (Gk.)
PHILIP — Alohalio, Lover of horses. (Gk.)
PHINEAS English form of Pinchas.
PIERCE Var. of Peter.
PIERRE French form of Peter.
PINCHAS — 'Ilimāku'e, Dark-complexioned. (Egypt.)
PIUS — Haipule, Devout. (L)

Q

QUENTIN — Kalima, The fifth (born). (L)
QUINCY Var. of Quentin.
QUINN Var. of Quentin.

R

RALPH — Kuauhāmakoa, Courageous advice. (Scand., OE)

RANDAL — Malupoʻokela, Superior protection. (OE)

RANDOLPH — Kuauhāmaikaʻi, Good counsel. (OE)

RAPHAEL English form of Refael.

RAY Dim. of Raymond.

RAYMOND — Maluhia, Quiet, peaceful. (G)

REFAEL — Olakeakua, God has healed. (H)

REGINALD — Naʻauao, Wise. (G)

RENE — Hānauhou, Reborn. (F)

REUBEN Var. of Reuven.

REUVEN — Aiahoʻihekamakāne; Behold, a son! (H)

REX — Mōʻī, King. (L) Dim. of Reginald.

REYNARD — Makoanaʻauao, Wisely bold. (G)

REYNOLD French form of Reginald.

RICHARD — Mōʻīmana, Strong king. (OF)

ROALD Dim. of Ronald.

ROBERT — Kaulanalaʻelaʻe, Bright fame. (G)

RODERICK — Mōʻīkaulana, Famous king. (G)

RODNEY — Kanakaanaʻāina, Surveyor. (OE)

RODOLP Var. of Rudolph.

ROGER — Koakaulana, Famous warrior. (OF)

ROLAND — Kaulanaokaʻāina, Fame of the land. (F, G)

ROLF Dim. of Rudolph.

ROLLO Dim. of Rudolph.

RONALD Scottish form of Reginald.

RORY — Hiʻohiʻo, Ruddy. (C) Irish form of Roderick.

ROSCOE — Liowiki, Swift horse. (OE)

ROSS — Kanahele, Woods. (OE)

ROY — Kamōʻī, King. (OF)

RUDOLPH Var. of Randolph, Ralph.

RUFUS — Lauohoʻula (For Caucasians), Lauohoʻehu (For Polynesians); Red haired. (L)

RUPERT Var. of Robert.

RUSSELL — Lauohoʻula (For Caucasians), Lauohoʻehu (For Polynesians); Rusty-haired. (OE)

S

SALOMON Var. of Solomon.

SAMSON English form of Shimshon.

SAMUEL — ʻOkeakuakonainoa, His name is God. (H)

SANDY Dim. of Alexander.

SAUL English form of Shaul.

SCHUYLER — Keauolo, Shelter. (Du.)

SCOTT — Kekākau; Scotsman, tattooed one. (L)

SEAMUS Irish form of James.

SEAN Irish form of John.

SEBASTIAN — Mōʻiuʻiu, Venerable. (Gk.)

SETH English form of Shet.

SEWARD — Kapalekahakai, Defender of the sea coast. (OE)

SEYMOUR — Nenelukai, Marsh lands near the seashore.(OE)

SHAUL — Nonoi, Asked. (H)

SHAWN Irish form of John.

SHELDON — Puʻupaleʻia, Protected hill. (OE)

SHET — Ponia; Appointed, ordained. (H) The third son of Adam.

SHIMON — Lohe, To hear. (H)

SHIMSHON — Kalā, The sun. (H)

SHIRLEY — Kulamauʻukuali, White meadow. (OE)

SIDNEY — Hoʻokalakupua, Enchanter. (Phoenician) Contraction of Saint Denys. See Dionysius.

SIEGFRIED — Malueo, Victorious peace. (G)

SIGISMUND — Malueo, Victorious protection. (G)

SIGMUND Var. of Sigismund.

SILAS — Nonoi; Latin form of the Aramaic and Hebrew, to ask.

SILVANUS — Ululā'au, Forest. (L)

SILVESTER Var. of Silvanus.

SIMEON English of Shimon.

SIMON Greek form of Shimon.

SINCLAIR — 'Alohi, Shining. (L)

SOLOMON — Maluhia, Peace. (H)

STANLEY — Kulapōhaku, Stony field. (OE)

STEPHEN — Leiali'i, Crown. (Gk.)

STEVEN Var. of Stephen.

STEWART — Kekahu, Guardian. (E)

SUMNER — 'Aulani, Messenger. (E)

SYDNEY Var. of Sidney.

SYLVANUS Var. of Silvanus.

SYLVESTER Var. of Silvanus.

T

TAFFY Welsh dim. of David.

TAD Dim. of Theodore or Thaddeus.

TED Dim. of Edward or Theodore.

TERENCE — Maika'i; Tender, good, gracious. (L)

THADEUS — Makanaokeakua, Gift of God. (Gk.)

THEOBALD — Lāhuikoa, Brave people. (G)

THEODORE — Makanaakua, Divine gift. (Gk.)

THEODORIC — Keli'iokalāhui, Ruler of the people. (G)

THEOPHILUS — Hiwahiwaakeakua, Beloved of God. (Gk.)

THOMAS — Māhoe, Twin. (Ar.)

TIMOTHY — Ho'ohanoikeakua, To honor God. (Gk.)

TITUS — Kanakanui, A person of great size and power. (L)

TOBIAS — Maika'ikeakua, God is good. (H)

TOD — Kapuo'a, Thicket. (E)

TONY Dim. of Anthony.

TRISTAN — Wawā; Noise, tumult. (C)

TYBALT Var. of Theobald.

U

ULYSSES Latin form of Odysseus, Greek king of Ithaca.

UMBERTO Italian form of Humbert.

URBAN — Kūlanakauhale, City. (L)

URIAH Var. of Uriya.

URIEL — 'Okeakuaku'ulama, God is my light. (H)

URIYA — 'Okeakuako'uula, God is my flame. Var. of Ur. (H)

UR — Ulaahi, Flame. (H)

V

VALENTINE — Kamaēhu; Strong, healthy. (L)

VAN — No, From (a particular city). Dutch form of the German 'von.'

VANCE — Kilohana, High point. (E)

VERGIL Var. of Virgil.

VERNON — Kupulau, Spring (season). (L)

VICTOR — Kana'i, Conqueror. (L)

VINCENT — Kana'i, Conqueror. (L)

VIRGIL — Hālupa, Flourishing. (L)

VIVIAN Masc. of Vivian.

W

WALDO — Ali'i, Ruler. (OE)

WALLACE — Malihini, Foreigner. (ME)

WALTER — 'Alihikaua, Ruler of the army. (OF)

WARD — Kahu, Guardian. (OE)

WARREN — Mālama, To preserve. (ME, OF)

WAYNE — Kulamau'u, Meadow. (E)

WEBB Dim. of Webster.

WEBSTER — Kanakaulana, Weaver. (OE)

WESLEY — Kulamau'ukomohana, West meadow. (OE)

WHITNEY — Haleali'ikea, White palace. (OE)

WILBUR — Lā'au'alohi (Bright tree), Bright willow. (OE)

WILFRED — Malukūpa'a, Resolute peace. (G)

WILLARD — Pālā'au (Yard of trees), Yard of willows. (E)

WILLIAM — Malukūpa'a, Resolute protection. (G)

WILLIS Son of William. See William.

WINFRED — Hoaalohamalu, Peaceful friend. (OE)

WINSTON — Hoapa'a, Secure friend. (OE)

WYATT — Wai, Water. (British)

X

XAVIER — Ho'ōla, Savior. (L) Name used by St. Francis.

XERXES — Kamō'ī, The king. (Per.)

Y

YALE — Kanakaho'oka'a, One who pays. (OE)

YEHOSHUA — 'Okeolakeakua, God is salvation. (H)

YOCHANAN — 'Olu'olukeakua, God is gracious. (H)

YORICK Possibly a Danish form of George. See Geofrey.

YORK Var. of Yorick.

YOSEF — Ho'olahakeakua, God will increase. (H)

YVES — Panapua, Archer. (Scand.) Var. of Ives.

YVON Var. of Ivan.

Z

ZACHARIAH Var. of Zecharya.

ZACHARY Var. of Zecharya.

ZEBEDEE — Makanaokeakua, Gift of God. (H)

ZECHARIAH Var. of Zecharya.

ZECHARYA — Ho'omana'o, Memory. (H)

ZEKE Dim. of Zecharya.

FEMININE — Wahine
A

ABIGAIL Var. of Avigayil.

ADA, ADAH — Kanani, Beauty. (H)

ADELA Var. of Adelaide.

ADELAIDE — Kūaliʻi, Nobility. (F)

ADELINE Dim. of Adelaide

ADRIENNE Fem. of Adrian. (F)

AGATHA — Maikaʻi, Good. (Gk.)

AGNES — Maʻemaʻe; Pure, sacred. (Gk.)

AIDA — Kōkua, To help. (L, OF)

AILEEN — Kalama, Light. (Gk.)

AIMEE — Kealoha, Love. (F, L)

ALBERTA Fem. of Albert.

ALETHEA — ʻOiaʻiʻo, Truth. (Gk.)

ALEXANDRA Fem. of Alexander.

ALEXIS Fem. of Alex.

ALFREDA Fem. of Alfred.

ALICE — Puaaliʻi, Noble birth. (ME)

ALICIA Var. of Alice.

ALIENOR French form of Eleanor.

ALINE Var. of Adeline.

ALISON — Kamaapuaaliʻi, Son of Alice. (Gmc.)

ALIX Dim. of Alexandra.

ALLEGRA — Hoʻolana, Cheerful. (L)

ALMA — Keohi, Maiden. (H)

ALMIRA — Kamāliʻiwahine, Princess. (Arb.)

ALPHONSINE Fem. of Alphonso.

ALTA — Loloa, Tall. (L)

ALTHEA — Hoʻōla, Healer. (Gk.)

ALVINA Fem. of Alvin.

AMABEL — Alohanani, Beautiful love. (L, F)

AMANDA — Aloha, To love. (L)

AMARINDA — Olamau, Long lived. (Gk., L)

AMELIA — Pa'ahana, Industrious. (H)

AMITY — Kealoha; Love, friendship. (L)

AMY Var. of Aimee.

ANASTASIA — Olahou, Resurrection. (Gk.)

ANDREA Fem. of Andrew.

ANGELA — 'Elele, Messenger. (Gk.)

ANGELICA Latin form of Angela.

ANITA Dim. of Anna.

ANN Var. of Anna.

ANNA Greek form of Chana.

ANNABEL — Lokomaika'inani, Beautifully gracious. Hybrid of Hebrew and Latin.

ANNETTE French form of Anna.

ANTHEA — Uluwehiwehi; Flowery, verdant. (Gk.)

ANTOINETTE — 'Ihi'ihi, Revered. (Gk., L)

ANTONIA Fem. of Anthony.

APRIL — Mōhala, To open. (L)

ARLENE Var. of Arline.

ARLINE — Kaikamahine, Girl. (G)

ASTERA — Hōkū, Star. (Per., Gk.)

ASTRID — Manalani, Divine strength. (Scand.) Also var. of Astera.

ATHENA — Na'auao, Wisdom. (Gk.)

AUDREY — Manaali'i, Noble strength. (OE)

AUGUSTA Fem. of Augustus.

AURELIA — Kalino (Shining, brilliant), Golden. (L)

AURORA — Wana'ao, Dawn. (L)

AVA — Manu, Bird. (L)

AVIGAYIL — 'Oka'oliku'umakua, My father is joy. (H)

AVIS — Pu'uhonua, Refuge in war. (G)

B

BABETTE French dim. of Elizabeth.

BAPTISTA Fem. of Baptist.

BARBARA — Malihini; Foreigner, stranger. (Gk.)

BATHSHEBA — Puaho'ohiki, Daughter of the promise. (H)

BEATA — Pōmaika'i, Blessed. (L)

BEATRICE — Kaho'opōmaika'i, She who brings blessings. (L)

BECKY Dim. of Rebecca.

BELINDA — Na'auao, Wise, (Gmc.)

BELLA Dim. of Arabella or Isabella.

BELLE — Kanani, Beautiful. (F)

BENEDICTA Fem. of Benedict.

BERENICE — Kaho'olanakila, The bringer of victory. (Gk.)

BERNADETTE Fem. of Bernard. (F)

BERNARDINE Fem. of Bernard. (F)

BERNICE Var. of Berenice.

BERTHA — Kaulana, Famous. (Gmc.)

BERYL — Pōhakumakamae, Precious stone. (Gk., Skt.)

BESS Dim. of Elizabeth.

BETH Dim. of Elizabeth.

BETHEL — Haleakua, House of God. (H)

BETSY Dim. of Elizabeth.

BETTINA Dim. of Elizabeth.

BETTY Dim. of Elizabeth.

BEULAH — Nohopili, Married. (H)

BIDDY Dim. of Bridget.

BLANCA — Ma'ema'e; Pure, unstained. (L)

BLANCHE Var. of Blanca.

BONNY — Maika'i, Good, (F, L)

BRENDA — Lauohouliuli, Dark haired. (C)

BRIDGET — Le'olani; High, lofty. (C)

C

CAMELLIA — Kapua; The flower, named after G. J. Kamel, 1661-1706, a Jesuit traveler. (NL)

CAMILLA — 'Ōhua; Servant, retainer. (L)

CANDACE — Ma'ema'e, Pure. (L)

CANDIDA Var. of Candace and Candice.

CARA Dim. of Caroline, See Caroline and Charlotte.

CARLA — Fem. of Charles. See Caroline and Charlotte.

CARLOTTA Italian form of Charlotte.

CARMEL — Kamāla, Garden. (H)

CARMEN Spanish form of Carmel.

CAROL — Kamele; Melody, song. (Glc.) See Caroline.

CAROLINE — Ikaika, Strong. (F) Fem. of Charles.

CASSANDRA — A'okāpae'ia, (One whose) warnings are ignored. (Gk.)

CATHERINE — Ma'ema'e, Pure. (Gk.)

CATHLEEN Var. of Kathleen and Catherine.

CECILIA Fem. of Cecil.

CELESTE — Kūlani, Heavenly. (F, L)

CELIA — Kūlani, Heavenly. (L)

CHANA — Lokomaika'i, Gracious. (H)

CHARISSA — Nani, Beauty. (Gk.)

CHARITY — Kealoha; Love, affection. (L)

CHARLENE Fem. of Charles. See Caroline.

CHARLOTTE — Ikaika, Strong. (F) Fem. of Charles.

CHEFTZI-BA — 'Oiaku'u'i'ini, She is my desire. (H)

CHERYL — Hiwahiwa, Beloved. (F)

CHLOE — Mōhala, Blooming. (Gk.)

CHRISTABEL — Kaponianani, The beautiful anointed one. (L)

CHRISTIANA Fem. of Christian.

CHRISTINA Var. of Christiana.

CHRISTINE Var. of Christina.

CICELY Var. of Cecilia.

CINDY Dim. of Cynthia and Lucinda.

CIS Dim. of Cecilia.

CLAIRE French form of Clara.

CLARA — ʻAlohi; Bright, clear. (L)

CLARABELLE — ʻAlohinani, Beautiful brightness. (L)

CLARICE Var. of Clara.

CLARINDA Var. of Clara.

CLAUDETTE Fem. of Claude.

CLAUDIA Fem. of Claude.

CLAUDINE Var. of Claudia.

CLEMENCE Fem. of Clement.

CLEMENTINE Fem. of Clement.

CLEOPATRA — Kapūhanoʻiaokaʻāina, Glorified of her country. (Gk.)

CLIO — Pūhano, Glorify. (Gk.)

CLOTILDA — Kaulanaikekaua, Famous in battle. (Gmc.)

COLETTE — Lanakila, Victorious. (L) Fem. dim. of Nicholas.

COLLEEN — Kamahine, Girl. (Irish)

CONSTANCE — Kūpaʻa; Constant, firm. (L)

CONSUELO — Hoʻonā, Consolation. (Sp.)

CORA — Kamahine, Maiden. (Gk.)

CORDELIA — Puakai (Sea flower), Daughter of the sea. (C)

CORINNA French form of Cora.

CORNELIA Fem. of Cornelius.

CRISTINA Italian and Spanish form of Christina.

CRYSTAL — Aniani, Clear. (Gk.)

CYNTHIA — Kamahina, The moon. (Gk.)

D

DAGMAR — Lāpāla'ela'e, Bright day. (G)

DAISY — Kamakaokalā, Eye of the day. (OE)

DALE — Awāwaiki, Small valley. (OE)

DAPHNE — Hōlio, Laurel tree. (Gk.)

DARLA — Meāloha, Beloved. (ME)

DARLEEN Dim. of Darla.

DAWN — Keao, Daybreak. (OE)

DEBORAH Var. of Devorah.

DEIRDRE — Kamahine, Young girl. (MI)

DELILAH — Lauoho, Hair. (H)

DELLA Var. of Adela.

DELPHINIA — Nai'a, Dolphin. (Gk.)

DENISE Fem. of Dennis.

DESIREE — Ka'i'ini, Desire. (F)

DEVORAH — Leolokomaika'i, Kind voice. (H)

DIANA — Ho'āno, Divine. (L)

DOLORES — Wahinekaumaha, Sorrowful woman. (L)

DOMINIQUE Fem. of Dominic.

DONNA — Wahineali'i, Lady of nobility. (L)

DORA Dim. of Dorothy, Eudora, or Theodora.

DORCAS — Kaohihiu, Gazelle. (Gk.)

DOREEN Dim. of Dorothy.

DORINDA See Belinda.

DORIS — Kahiau, To give bountifully. (Gk.)

DOROTHY — Makanaakua, Gift of God. (Gk.)

DRUSILLA — Ho'oikaika, She who strengthens. (L)

DULCIE — Māhie; Sweet, charming. (L)

DULCINEA — Māhie, Sweet one. (Sp.)

E

EDITH — Kū'ono'ono, Prosperous. (OE)

EDNA — 'Ano'i; Delight, desired, adorned, voluptuous. (H.)
EDWINA Fem. of Edwin.
EFFIE Dim. of Euphemia.
EILEEN Irish form of Helen.
EKATERINA Russian form of Catherine.
ELAINE Var. of Helen.
ELBERTA Fem. of Elbert.
ELEANOR Var. of Helen.
ELECTRA — Ke'alohi, Shining one. (Gk.)
ELENA Var. of Helen.
ELISHEVA — 'Okeakuaka'uho'ohiki, God is my oath. (H)
ELIZA Dim. of Elizabeth.
ELIZABETH English form of Elisheva.
ELLA Dim. of Eleanor.
ELLEN Var. of Helen.
ELOISA — Italian form of Louise.
ELOISE Var. of Louise.
ELSA Dim. of Elizabeth.
ELSPETH Scottish form of Elizabeth.
ELVA — Meaiki, Elf. (OE)
ELVIRA — Panipono, To close completely. (Sp., G.)
EMELINE Var. of Emily.
EMERALD — Pōhaku'ōma'o, Green stone. (OE)
EMILY — Pa'ahana, Industrious. Fem. of Emil.(L)
EMMA — Kupunawahine, Grandmother. (OE)
ENID — Keola, Life. (C)
ERICA Fem. of Eric.
ERMA — Dim. of Ermengarde.
ERMENGARDE — Kahunui, Great guardian. (Gmc.)
ERMENTRUDE — Ikaikanui, Great strength. (Gmc.)
ERNESTINE Fem. of Ernest.

ESMERALDA Spanish form of Emerald.
ESTELLE Spanish of Esther.
ESTHER — Kahōkū, Star. (Per.)
ETHEL — Keliʻi, Noble. (OE)
ETTA Dim. of Henrietta.
EUDORA — Makanamaikaʻi, Good gift. (Gk.)
EUGENIA Fem. of Eugene.
EULALIA — ʻŌlelomaikaʻi, Good talk. (Gk.)
EUNICE — Lanakilahauʻoli, Happy victory. (Gk.)
EUPHEMIA — ʻŌlelomaikaʻi, Good speech. (Gk.)
EVA Var. of Eve.
EVANGELINE — ʻElele, Messenger. (Gk.)
EVE — Keola, Life. (H)
EVELYN Dim. of Eve.
EVITA Spanish form of Eve.

F

FAITH — Paulelekūpaʻa, Unswerving trust. (OE)
FANNY Dim. of Frances.
FAUSTINA — Pōmaikaʻi, Lucky. (L)
FAWN — Makalauna, Friendly. (L)
FAY — Kūpaʻa, Fidelity. (OF)
FELICIA — Hauʻoli, Happy. (L)
FERN — Kekoa, Brave. (OE)
FERNANDA Fem. of Fernando, Spanish form of Ferdinand.
FIDELIA — Kūpaʻa, Faithful. (L)
FIONA — ʻIlikea; Fair, white. (C)
FLAVIA — Keohohākea, Blonde. (L)
FLORA — Kapua, Flower. (L)
FLORENCE — Kupuohi, Blooming. (L)
FRANCES Fem. of Francis.

FRANCINE Dim. of Frances.

FREDERICA Fem. of Frederick.

FRIEDA — Maluhia, Peace. (G)

G

GABRIELLE Fem. of Gabriel.

GAIL Dim. of Abigail.

GAY — Hauʻoli, Merry. (OE)

GENEVIEVE — Nalukea, White wave. (F, C)

GENEVRA Var. of Guinevere.

GEORGIA Fem. of George.

GEORGIANA Fem. of George.

GERALDINE Fem. of Gerald.

GERMAINE — Polapola; Sprout, bud. (ME, L)

GERTRUDE — Kamahinekaua, Battle maid. (Gmc.)

GILBERTA Fem. of Gilbert.

GILDA — ʻŌhuaakeakua, Servant of God. (C)

GILLIAN — Kamahine, Girl. (OE) Var. of Juliana.

GINEVRA Var. of Guinevere.

GINGER — ʻAwapuhi, Ginger plant. (OF) Dim. of Virginia.

GIOVANNA Fem. of Giovanni, Italian form of John.

GISELE — Manaʻolanaʻalohi, Bright hope. (OE)

GIULIA Italian form of Julia.

GLADYS — ʻĀlohilohi, Brilliant. (C)

GLENNA Fem. of Glenn.

GLORIA — Hanohano, Glory. (L)

GRACE — Kealoha, Grace. (L)

GRETA Swedish dim. of Margaret.

GRETCHEN German dim. of Margaret.

GRISELDA — ʻĀhinahina, Gray. (F)

GUINEVERE — Nalukea, White wave. (C)

GUSSIE Fem. dim. of Augustus.

GWEN — Pōmaika'inani, Beautifully blessed. (Wel.)

GWENDOLYN Dim. of Gwen.

GWENETH — Pōmaika'i, Fair or blessed. (Wel.)

GWN Var. of Gwen.

H

HANNAH Var. of Chana.

HARRIET Fem. of Harry.

HAZEL — Lā'aumana, Tree of authority. (OE)

HEATHER — La'alā'au, Shrub. (OE)

HEDDA — Kaua, War. (Gmc.)

HEDWIG — Kaua, War. (Gmc.)

HEFZIBA English form of Cheftzi-Ba.

HELEN — Malama; Light, a torch. (Gk.)

HELENA Var. of Helen.

HELGA — Hemolele, Holy. (Gmc.)

HELOISE French form of Eloise, fem. of Louis.

HENRIETTA Fem. of Henry.

HEPHZIBAH Var. of Hefziba.

HERMIONE Fem. of Hermes.

HESTER Var. of Esther.

HETTY Dim. of Esther, Henrietta, or Hester.

HILARY — Hau'oli, Joyful. (L)

HILDA — Kamahinekaua, Battle maiden. (OE)

HILDEGARDE — Kamahinekia'ikaua, Guardian battle maiden. (Gmc.)

HOLLY — Hemolele, Holy . (OE)

HONORA — Ho'ohano, Honor. (L)

HOPE — Mana'olana, Trust. (OE)

HORTENSE — Mahi'ai, Gardener. (L)

HYACINTH — Pōhakuponi, Purplish gem. (Gk.)

I

IDA — Hau'oli, Happy. (Gk.)

ILONA — Ha'ikūke'oke'o (Silver oak tree), Oak tree. (H)

ILSE Var. of Elizabeth.

IMOGENE — Keaka; Image, likeness. (L)

INA — Makuahine, Mother. (L) Dim. of Eugenia.

INEZ — Ma'ema'e, Pure. (Gk., Pg.) Var. Portuguese form of Agnes.

IRENE — Maluhia, Peace. (Gk.)

IRIS — Ānuenue, Rainbow. (Gk.)

IRMA Var. of Erma.

ISABEL Var. of Elisabeth.

ISADORA Fem. of Isidore.

IVY — Lā'auhihi, Vine. (ME)

J

JACQUELINE Fem. of Jacques, French form of Jacob.

JANE Fem. of John. See Johanna.

JANET Dim. of Jane.

JANICE Dim. of Jane.

JEAN Scottish form of Johanna.

JEANNE French form of Johanna.

JEANNETTE Dim. of Jeanne.

JEMIMA English form of Yemima.

JENNIFER Var. of Guinevere.

JERRY Dim. of Geraldine.

JESSICA Fem. of Jesse.

JEWEL — Hau'oli, Joy. (OF)

JILL Dim. var. of Julia. Dim. of Gillian.

JO Dim. of Josephine.

JOAN Var. of Johanna.

JOCELYN German fem. of Jacob.

JOHANNA German and English form of Yochana, fem. of Yochanan.

JOSEPHA Fem. var. of Joseph.

JOSEPHINE French fem. of Joseph.

JOY Dim. of Joyce.

JOYCE — Hau'oli, Joyful. (L)

JUANA Spanish form of Johanna.

JUANITA Spanish dim. of Juana.

JUDITH English form of Yehudit.

JULIA Fem. of Julius.

JULIANA Fem. of Julian.

JULIET Dim. of Julia.

JUNE — U'imau, Ever youthful. (L)

JUSTINA Fem. of Justin.

K

KAREN Danish form of Katherine.

KATE Dim of Katherine.

KATHERINE — Ma'ema'e, Purity. (Gk.) Var. of Catherine.

KATHLEEN Irish form of Catherine.

KATHY Dim. of Katherine.

KATY Dim. of Katherine.

KAY Dim. of Katherine.

KIRSTEN Norwegian form of Christine.

KITTY Dim. of Katherine.

KLARA German form of Clara.

L

LAURA — Hōlio, Laurel tree. (L)

LAURETTA Dim. of Laura.

LAURINDA Var. of Laura.

LAVERNE — La'aulu, Spring time. (L, F)

LEAH — Māluhiluhi, To be weary. (H)

LEILA — Kanani'ilikou, The dark-skinned beauty. (Arb.)

LENA Dim. of Helena.

LENORA Var. of Eleanor.

LEONA Fem. of Leo and Leon.

LEONORA Var. of Eleanor.

LEORA Var. of Leonora.

LESLIE From the masc. Leslie.

LETITIA — Hau'oli, Joy. (L)

LIBBY Dim. of Elizabeth.

LINDA — Kanani, Pretty. (Sp.) Dim. of Belinda or Melinda.

LISA Dim. of Elizabeth.

LISETTE French dim. of Elizabeth.

LIZBETH Dim. of Elizabeth.

LIZZIE Dim. of Elizabeth.

LOIS — Maika'i, Desireable. (Gk.)

LOLA Dim. of Dolores.

LORENE Var. of Laura.

LORETTA Dim. of Laura.

LORINDA Var. of Laurinda.

LORNA — Kalilo, Lost (OE)

LORRAINE Var. of Laura.

LOTTIE Dim. of Charlotte.

LOUELLA Var. of Luella.

LOUISE Fem. of Louis.

LUCIA Fem. of Lucius.

LUCILLE Var. of Lucia.

LUCINDA Var. of Lucia.

LUCRETIA Fem. of Lucretius.

LUCY Var. of Lucia.

LUELLA Derived from Louise and Ella.
LUISA Italian form of Louisa.
LULU Dim. of Louise.
LURLEEN — Pūkaua, War horn. (Scand.)

M

MABEL — Ku'unani, My beautiful one. (L) Dim. of Annabel.
MADGE Dim. of Margaret.
MAE — Dim. of Mary and Margaret.
MAG Dim. of Margaret.
MAISIE Dim. of Margaret.
MALVINA Fem. var. of Melvin.
MAMIE Dim. of Margaret.
MANDY Dim. of Amanda.
MARCELLA Fem. of Marcellus.
MARCIA Fem. of Marcius, var. of the masc. Marcus.
MARGARET — Momi, Pearl. (Gk.)
MARGARITA Italian and Spanish form of Margaret.
MARGE Dim. of Margery.
MARGERY Var. of Margaret.
MARGOT Var. of Margaret.
MARGUERITE Var. of Margaret.
MARIA Var. of Mary.
MARIAN Var. formed from Mary and Anne.
MARIANNE Formed from Mary and Anne.
MARIE French form of Mary.
MARIETTA Dim. of Maria.
MARILYN Var. of Mary.
MARION Var. of Mary.
MARJORIE Var. of Margaret.
MARSHA Var. of Marcia.

MARTHA — Kawahine; Woman, mistress. (Ar.)

MARY Greek form of the Hebrew, Miryam (Miriam).

MATHILDA — Kamahinekauanui, Mighty battle maid. (Gmc.)

MATILDA Var. of Mathilda.

MAUD French dim. of Mathilda.

MAURA Irish form of Mary.

MAUREEN Dim. of Maura.

MAVIS — 'Āmauimele, Song-thrush. (OE)

MAXINE Fem. of Maximilian.

MEG Dim. of Margaret.

MEGAN Welsh form of Margaret.

MELANIE — Pō'ele, Black. (Gk.)

MELINDA — Mālie, Gentle. (Gk. OE)

MERCEDES — Kealoha, Mercy. (L)

MERCY — Kealoha; Mercy, pity. (L)

META Dim. of Margaret.

MIGNON — Lahilahi, Delicate. (F)

MILDRED — Leomālie, Gentle speech. (OE)

MILLICENT — Melehone, Sweet singer. (L)

MIMI French dim. of Miryam.

MINA Dim. of Wilhelmina.

MINNA Dim. of Wilhelmina.

MINNIE Dim. of Miryam and Wilhelmina.

MIRANDA — Kamaha'o, Wonderful. (L)

MIRIAM Var. of Miryam.

MIRYAM — Kailu'ulu'u, Sea of sorrow. (H) Var. of Mary.

MOIRA Var. of Maura.

MOLLY Dim. of Miryam.

MONA — Kalani, Noble. (Irish).

MORNA — Hiwahiwa, Beloved. (C, Glc.)

MURIEL — Hau'oli, Merry. (ME)

MYRA Var. of Moira.
MYRNA Var. of Morna.
MYRTLE — Maile, Myrtle plant. (Per.)

N

NADA — Mana'olana, Hope. (Slavic)
NADINE French form of Nada.
NAN Dim. of Ann.
NANCY Dim. of Ann.
NANNETTE Dim. of Ann.
NAOMI — Māhie, Delightful. (H)
NATALIE — Hānau, To be born. (L)
NELL Dim. of Eleanor, Ellen or Helen.
NETTIE Dim. of Antoinette, Henrietta, or Jeannette.
NICOLE French form of the masc. Nicholas.
NINA Dim. of Ann.
NITA Dim. of Juanita.
NONA — Kaiwa, Ninth. (L)
NORA Dim. of Eleanor, Honora, Leonora.
NOREEN Irish dim. of Nora.
NORMA — Maluhia, Peaceful.

O

OCTAVIA Fem. of Octavius.
OLGA — Hemolele, Holy. (Russ., Scand.)
OPAL — Pōhakumakamae, Jewel. (Skt.)
OPHELIA — Kōkua, Help. (Gk.)
OTTILIE Swedish fem. var. of Otto.

P

PAMELA — Kaipo, A name invented by Sir Philip Sidney meaning 'loved one.' (Gk., OE)
PANSY — Mana'o, To think. (F)

PATIENCE — Ahonui, Patience. (L)

PATRICIA Fem. of Patrick.

PAULA Fem. of Paul.

PAULETTE Var. fem. dim. of Paul.

PAULINE French fem. dim. of Paul.

PEARL — Momi, Pearl. (L, ME)

PEG Dim. of Margaret.

PEGGY Dim. of Margaret.

PENELOPE — Hanakaiāmū, Silent worker. (Gk.)

PHILIPPA Fem. of Phillip.

PHOEBE — ʻAlohi, Bright, shining. (Gk.)

PHYLLIS — Lauʻōmaʻo, Green bough or leaf. (Gk.)

POLLY Var. of Molly.

POPPY — Puakala, Poppy plant. (L)

PORTIA — Puaʻa, Hog. (L)

PRISCILLA — Kahiko, Ancient. (L)

PRUDENCE — Akahele; Prudent, cautious. (L)

Q

QUEENIE — Mōʻīwahine, Queen. (L) Dim. of Regina.

R

RAMONA Fem. of Ramon, Spanish form of Raymond.

REBA Dim. of Rebecca.

REBECCA — Hīkiʻi; To tie, bind. (H)

REGINA — Mōʻīwahine, Queen. (L)

RENATA — Hānauhou, Reborn. (L)

RENEE French form of Renata.

RHEA — Hoʻomaluonākūlanakauhale, Protector of cites. (Gk.)

RITA — Kūpono, Honest. (Skt.) Dim. of Margarita.

ROBERTA Fem. of Robert.

ROBIN Dim. of Roberta.

ROCHELLE — 'Ili'ili, Small stone. (OF)

RONNY Dim. of Veronica.

ROSAMOND — Ho'omaluokalio, Protector of the horse. (Gmc.)

ROWENA — Lauohokeamōhala, Flowering white hair. (C)

ROXANA — Keao, Dawn of day. (Per.)

RUBY — Ka'ula, Red, reddish. (L, F)

RUTH — Pilialoha, Friendship. (H)

S

SADIE Dim. of Sarah.

SALLY Dim. of Sarah.

SALOME — Maluhia, Peaceful. (H)

SANDRA Dim. of Alexandra.

SARAH — Kamāli'iwahine, Princess. (H)

SELMA — 'Ilikea, Fair. (C)

SERENA — Maluhia, Peaceful. (L)

SHARON — Kekula; Plain, flat area. (H)

SHEILA Irish form of Cecilia.

SHIRLEY — Kulamau'ukea, White meadow. (OE)

SIBYL — Kāulawahine, Prophetess. (Gk.)

SIGRID Fem. of Siegfried.

SILVIA Var. of Sylvia.

SIMONE French fem. of Simon.

SOFIA German, Italian, and Swedish form of Sophia.

SONIA Russian dim. of Sophia.

SOPHIA — Na'auao, Wise. (Gk.)

SOPHRONIA — Akahele, Prudent. (Gk.)

STACIE Dim. of Anastasia.

STELLA — Kahōkū, Star. (L)

STEPHANIE Fem. of Stephen.

SYBIL Var. of Sibyl.

SYLVIA — Kanahele, The forest. (L)
SYDNEY Fem. of Sidney.

T

TABITHA — Kaohihiu, Gazelle. (Ar.)
TERESA Var. of Theresa.
THALIA — Hālupa, Flourishing. (Gk.)
THEA Dim. of Althea.
THELMA Var. of Selma.
THEODORA Fem. of Theodore.
THEODOSIA — Makanaakua, Divine gift. (Gk.)
THERESA — Kameaʻohi, She who reaps. (Gk.)
TILDA Dim. of Matilda.
TILLY Dim. of Matilda.
TINA Dim. of Christina.
TRIXIE Dim. of Beatrice or Beatrix.
TRUDY Dim. of Gertrude.

U

UNA — Kekahi, The one. (L)
UNDINE — Kanalu, The wave. (L)
UNITY Var. of Una.
URANIA — Kalani, The heaven. (Gk.)

V

VALENTINE — Olakinomaikaʻi, Healthy. (L)
VALERIA — Hoʻolehua, Strong. (L)
VANESSA — Pulelehua, Butterfly. (Gk.)
VENUS — Aloha, To love. (L)
VERA — Kaʻoiaʻiʻo, Truth. (L) or Paulele, Faith. (Russ.)
VERONICA — ʻOiaʻiʻo, Truthful. (L)
VI Dim. of Violet and Victoria.

VICKI Var. of Victoria.
VICTORIA — Lanakila, Victory. (L)
VIOLA — Naniwaiʻaleʻale, Violet. (L)
VIOLET Var. of Viola.
VIRGILIA Fem. of Virgil.
VIRGINIA — Maʻemaʻe, Pure. (L)
VIVIAN — Ola, Alive. (L)

W

WANDA — Kaʻauana, Wanderer. (OE)
WENDY Dim. of Gwendolyn.
WENCNA — Hauʻoli, Joy. (OE)
WILHELMINA German form of William.
WILLA Dim. of Wilhelmina.
WILMA Dim. of Wilhelmina.
WINIFRED Fem. of Winfred.

Y

YEHUDIT — Mililani, Praise. (H)
YEMIMA — Manukū, Dove. (Arb.)
YOLANDA — Makahilahila; Modest, shy. (L) Keao, Dawn. (Gk.) Old French var. of Viola.
YVETTE Fem. of Yves.
YVONNE Fem. of Yves.

Z

ZAZA — Keau, Movement. (H)
ZENOBIA — Hoʻailona; Sign, symbol. (Gk.)
ZOE — Keola, Life. (Gk.)

BIBLIOGRAPHY

Kolatch, Alfred J. *The Complete Dictionary of English and Hebrew First Names.* New York: Jonathan David Publishers, Inc., 1984.

"Laws of His Majesty, Kamehameha IV." Archives of Hawaii, 1860.

Pūku'i, Mary Kawena, and Samuel H. Elbert. *Hawaiian Dictionary*, Hawaiian-English, English-Hawaiian. Honolulu: University of Hawaii Press, 1971.

Pūku'i, Mary Kawena, E. W. Haertig, and Catherine A. Lee. *Nānā I Ke Kumu* (Look To The Source), Vols. I-II. Honolulu: Hui Hānai, 1972, 1979.

Pūku'i, Mary Kawena, Samuel H. Elbert, and Esther T. Mo'okini. *Place Names of Hawaii.* Honloulu: University Press of Hawaii, 1974.

Pūku'i, Mary Kawena, and Samuel H. Elbert. *Hawaiian Grammar.* Honolulu: University of Hawaii Press, 1979.

The Reader's Digest Great Encyclopedic Dictionary. New York: The Reader's Digest Association, Inc., 1966.

Session Laws of Hawaii, 4th State Legislature. Archives of Hawaii, 1967.